Lovesickness Letizia Laford
- count me out!
Scribble Book, Fill-in Book and Colouring Book

First edition 2017

© 2017 Letizia Laford
Cover, translation and design by Letizia Laford
Cover image with images from veekicl (#117245047, #178395016, #163103909, #163103946, #180008506, #175980215, #175102746) / fotolia
Layout with images from veekicl (#117245047, #178395016, #163103909, #163103946, #180008506, #175980215, #175102746) / fotolia & yasnaten (#117245047) / fotolia
Printed and published by: BoD – Books on Demand, Norderstedt.
ISBN: 978-3-746-04750-8

Important note about this book

You take full responsibility for your actions.
This book does not replace a visit to a doctor or psychotherapist.

I can not promise that the content of this book will actually help you in your current situation. You have to find your way through your grief yourself.

If you are currently undergoing medical treatment, please talk to your doctor in advance.

I am your book!

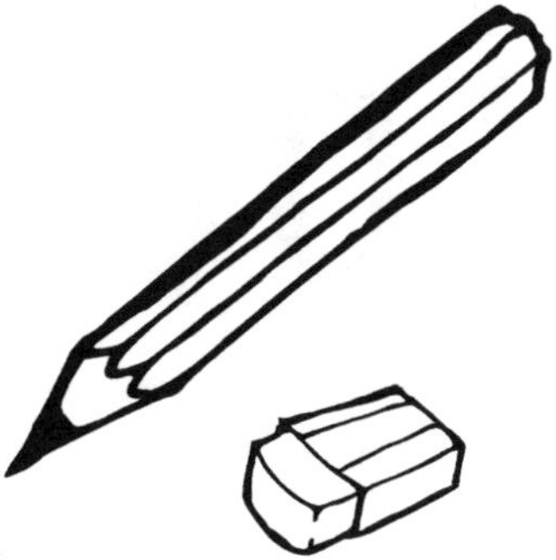

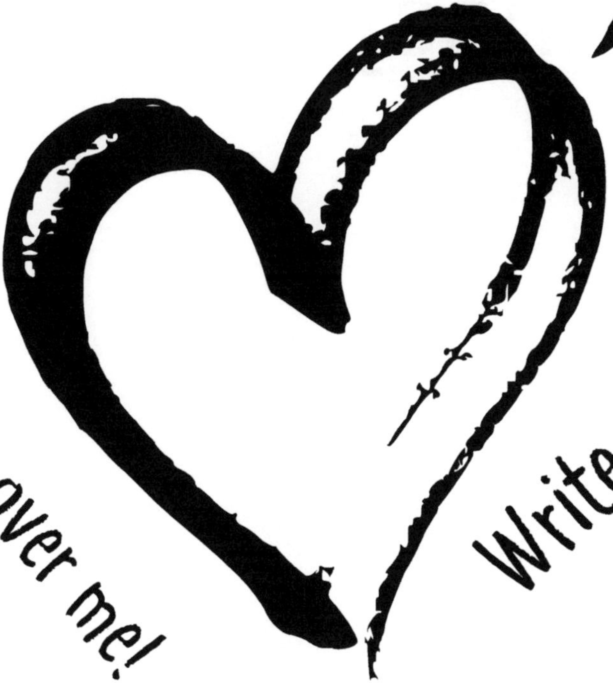

Scribble over me!

Write in me!

Colour me in!

Lovesickness

[ˈlʌvsɪknəs]

1. unrequited love
2. horrible pains
3. You can not judge if you
have never experienced it.

Dear lovesick reader,

This Scribble Book / Fill-in Book / Colouring Book is especially for you to deal with your lovesickness. It does not matter if you have a painful separation behind you or the object of your desire is unattainable for you.

This book is to help you cope better with your grief. Because it is important to give room to your heartbreak. This space is offered by the 112 pages of this book.

You can start on each page with your lovesickness. Likewise, you can always return to a page if you want to add something. If you do not feel able to master a particular task, do it another day.

You may only fill in the last pages of this book if you have overcome your lovesickness.

Your Letizia

My name is

_____

and since _____ . . _____ I am
lovesick because of _____,
whom I cannot have because

_____

_____

_____

_____

_____

First aid

Your heartache is still fresh

It feels awful and you have the feeling that you cannot live without him. These first days and weeks are the worst.

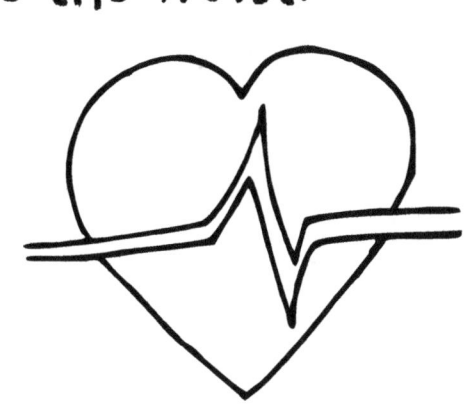

But you will do it!
He will not let you down but regret that you are not his partner (anymore).

1st step

Get a big box and put everything in it that reminds you of him:

- Photos
- Gifts
- Clothes
- Letters
  etc.

Hide the box in the basement.

2nd step

Cancel the contact:

- Delete his contact information.

- Unfriend him on Facebook & Co.

- Do not answer his contact attempts.

The 1st month

Today is the ___ . . ___ and you
are feeling _____ .

How are you now?

_____

_____

_____

_____

_____

_____

_____

Where is your pain and how strong is it?

The 1st month

When did you last contact him? How did it go?

_____

_____

_____

_____

_____

_____

_____

_____

When did you last see him? How was it?

_____

_____

_____

_____

_____

When did you last think of him?
How often do you still think of him?

_____

_____

_____

His opinion does not count!

He does not like you, so what?

You are beautiful.
You are awesome.
You are intelligent.
You are desirable.
You are unique.

He does not deserve you!

You are important!

In your life, only what you want counts. What are your goals for your life without him?

_____

_____

_____

_____

_____

_____

_____

Life goes on

Find a new hobby:

- Creative activities like painting, writing or crafting calms down.

- Sport provides balance.

- Skydiving and similar activities give you a very special thrill.

Not again ...

Do not jump into the next adventure directly! He would think you are a bitch. You do not want that!

Men should stay away from you.

You may!

It's OK to be in love.
It's OK to mourn.
It's OK to be in a bad mood.
It's OK to miss him.
It's OK to take a day off.
It's OK if you're happy without him.
It's OK if you hate him.
It's OK not to put up with everything.
It's OK to take the time you need.

You should not!

It is not OK to stalk him.
It is not OK to blame him.
It is not OK to insult him.
It is not OK to seek contact with him.
It is not OK to idealize him.
It is not OK to judge you.
It is not OK to hurt him.
It's not OK to give up on you.
It's not OK not to let him go.

Every beginning is difficult

What do you want to avoid
when dealing with him? Write it
down and remember it again and again.

_____

_____

_____

_____

_____

_____

_____

Without him, your life is colorful

Give him a name

If you talk with your friends about him, you should give him a name that does not match his first name. If you do not have one yet, you will find a selection of suitable substitute names for the man who broke your heart on the next page.

Tick your choice!

- [ ] asshole
- [ ] dumbass
- [ ] idiot
- [ ] monkey
- [ ] douchebag
- [ ] namby-pamby
- [ ] wimp
- [ ] motherfucker
- [ ] pig
- [ ]

This idiot!

He is a monster!

You always knew it.
Paint him in all his ugliness!

Other mothers ...

... also have beautiful sons.

Be open to a flirtation. You will see:
There are many great men and some
are even totally on you.

Who needs him anymore???

He is a bad partner

Why would you advise others against a relationship with him?

"Pleasure of love
lasts but a moment.
Pain of love lasts a
lifetime."

Jean-Pierre Claris de Florian

Love is a gift

Give your love only

to someone who

appreciates it.

What does he not have that will mark your next partner?

_____

_____

_____

_____

_____

_____

_____

_____

_____

_____

I cannot do this!

If you can not banish him completely from your life and you cannot cope with it, that's OK.

Move, change your job or school.

Otherwise you will not get away from him!

You are not an option!

Do not let him persuade you.

If he does not want you now, then he won't want you later either.

Tell him if he does not leave you alone!

This always helps

Get in front of the TV:

- Grab ice cream, cake, popcorn: whatever your heart desires.

- Watch the best love movies you know.

- Let your tears run wild.

You are the best!

Lovesickness is the perfect occasion to become a workaholic.

Who says money does not make you happy?

Whom? ... oh, him!

Avoid any contact with him because that could further fuel your grief.

- Avoid him.

- Do not visit his online profiles.

- Do not call him.

Yeah, he doesn't want me!

Why is it good that you are not a couple? Write it down and never forget it!

_____

_____

_____

_____

_____

_____

_____

„Often, one sees only too late, how much he was loved, how forgetful and ungrateful he was, and how great the unrecognized heart was."

Jean Paul

„To forget someone means to think of him."

Jean de La Bruyère

He is a complete idiot!
What are the dumbest
things he has ever said
to you?

Tell everyone!

OMG

Your friends do not want to hear about it anymore, but you should talk about your grief.

Tell the whole world via social media or blog.

Stay fair and do not insult him!

Your lifebelt

Everyone needs a lifebelt – whatever makes you feel good. What is yours? Write it in the lifebelt.

Hiking

Shopping

Talking to my mother

Dancing

Reading

My dog

Chocolate

Party with friends

It does not get better!

If you cannot go on:

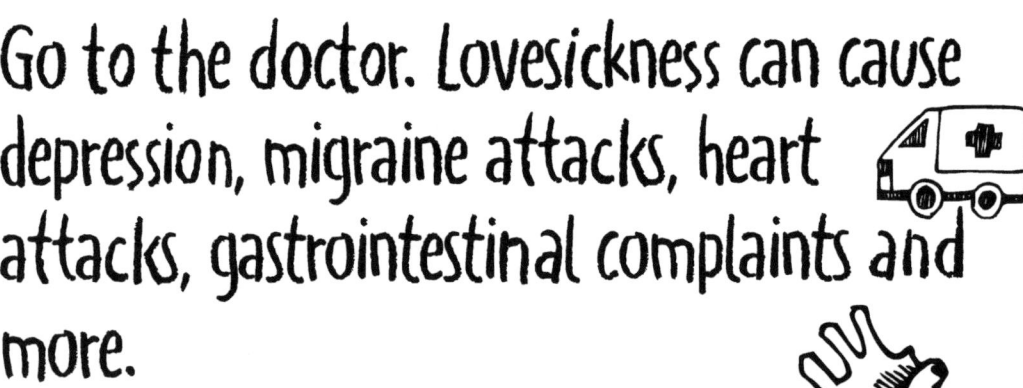

Go to the doctor. Lovesickness can cause depression, migraine attacks, heart attacks, gastrointestinal complaints and more.

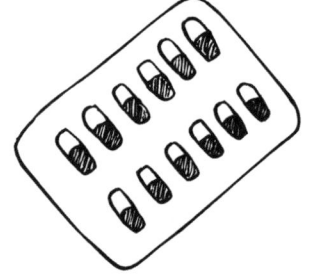

Spill it out!

Write him a letter in which you write everything you have always wanted to tell him. Tell him everything you would not talk about.

Do not send the letter!

Give yourself a break!

Go on vacation & visit a place you have never been to. The new impressions will blow you away.

Take a friend with you or enjoy the time alone.

By the way: holidays do not have to be expensive!

He is a bottle

Label the bottle so everyone knows why to stay away from him / it.

Wounds can heal.
Scars will stay.

Your future will be great

Write about how your future will develop positively without him.

_____

_____

_____

_____

_____

_____

_____

"Tears clean the heart."

Fjodor Michailowitsch Dostojewski

Crying is OK!

Lovesickness is usually a terrible torture. It is perfectly fine to feel bad and cry. Because only what we have mourned, we can leave behind us.

More time for you

Think less about him and use the time for beautiful moments or your own projects instead.

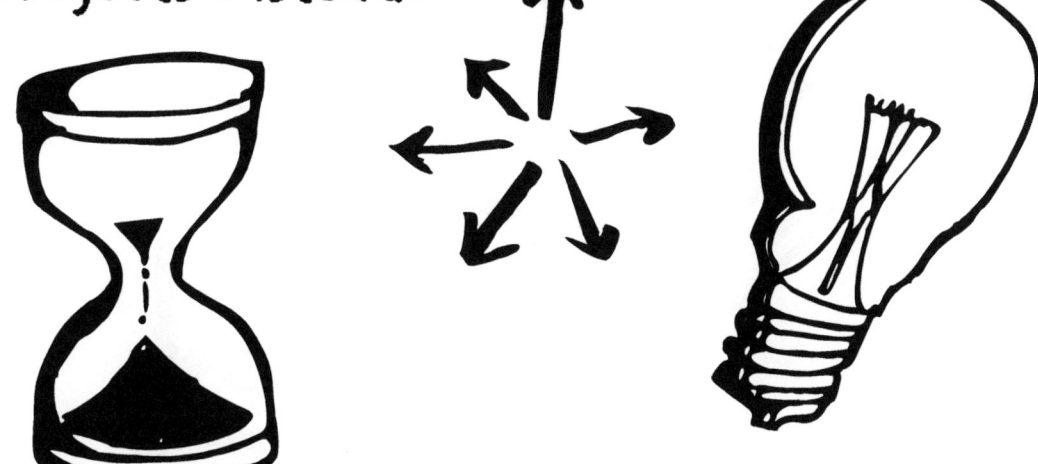

You do not need him to be complete!

„Whom you love the most, you hurt the easiest."

Fjodor Michailowitsch Dostojewski

Love letter for you

Write a love letter to yourself! You need someone to caress your soul and tell you how great you are.

_____

_____

_____

_____

_____

_____

↵

„The grief that does not speak knits up the o-er wrought heart and bids it break."

William Shakespeare

You really like him.
But nobody is perfect.

What do you dislike about him?

_____
_____

_____

_____

_____

_____

_____

The 3rd month

Today is the ___. ___. ___ and you are feeling _____ .

How are you now?

_____

_____

_____

_____

_____

_____

Where is your pain and how strong is it?

The 3rd month

When did you last contact him? How did it go?

_____

_____

_____

_____

_____

_____

_____

_____

When did you last see him? How was it?

_____

_____

_____

_____

_____

When did you last think of him?
How often do you still think of him?

_____

_____

_____

What can he not give you?

If he is not with you, he is not the right one!

He is terrible

Which bad qualities does he combine?

_____

_____

_____

_____

_____

_____

_____

_____

That always helps

A day in the city:

- Go shopping and buy yourself something you've been wanting for a long time.

- Enjoy the beautiful weather in the park, cafe, etc.

- Make you feel good about yourself, e.g. with a new hairstyle.

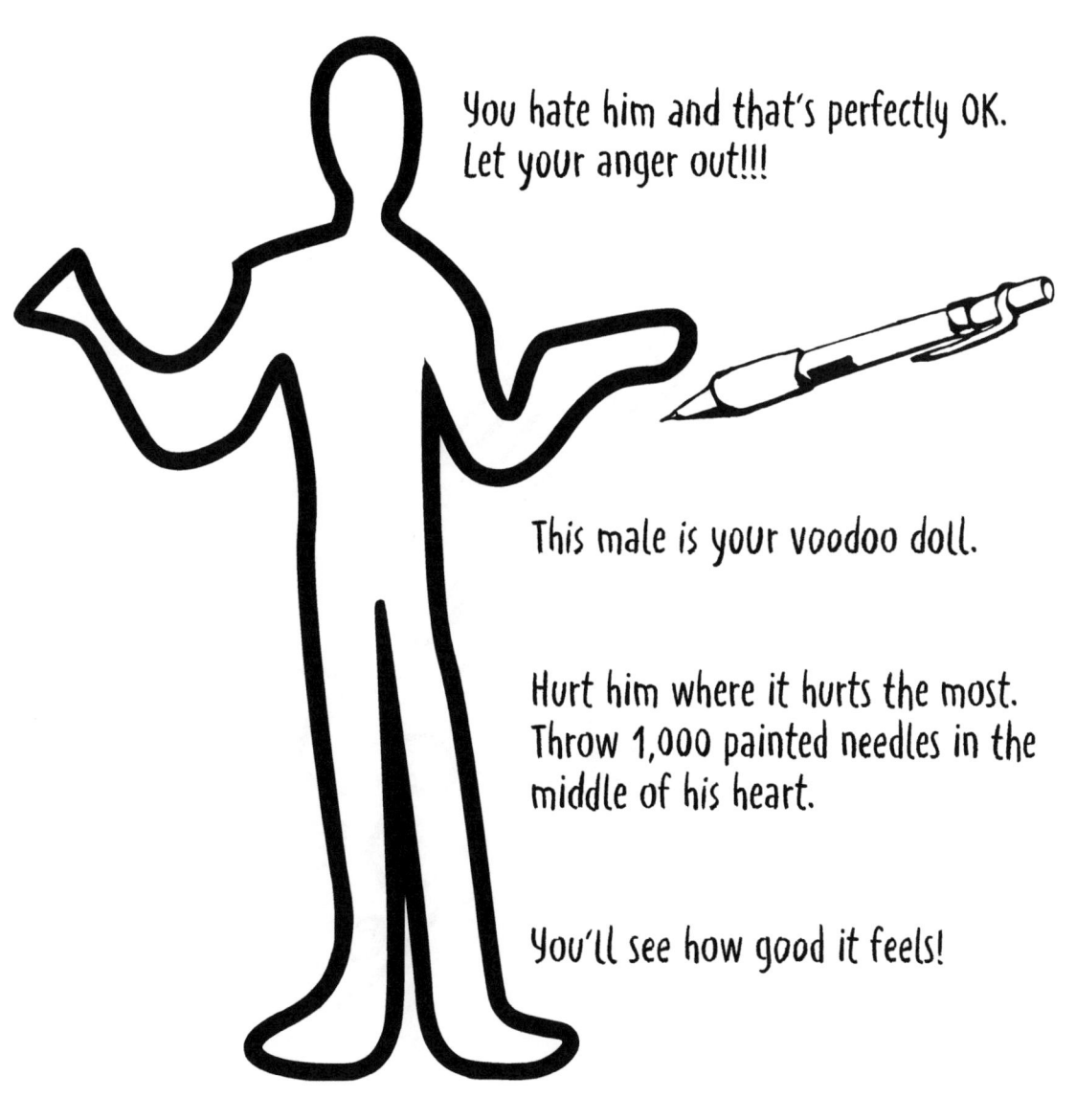

You are a princess. He is only a subject.

Why are you too good for him?

No time!

Fill your schedule!

As long as you are busy, you have no chance to think about him.

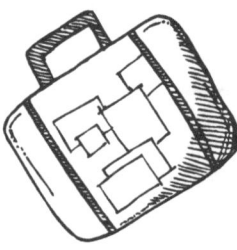

Your friends know exactly:
He is not good for you.

What do you want from him?

Why do they think he is lousy?

_____

_____

_____

_____

_____

_____

_____

He is an animal

Which one? Why?

_____

_____

_____

_____

_____

_____

_____

_____

_____

The 6th month

Today is the _____ . _____ . _____ and you
are feeling _____ .
How are you now?

_____

_____

_____

_____

_____

_____

_____

Where is your pain and how strong is it?

The 6th month

When did you last contact him?
How did it go?

_____

_____

_____

_____

_____

_____

_____

_____

When did you last see him?
How was it?

_____

_____

_____

_____

When did you last think of him?
How often do you still think of him?

_____

_____

_____

Sometimes love is like cats.
It does not want to cuddle but scratch.

Moodbooster

What do you want to spend more time doing? Write down everything you enjoy.

_____

_____

_____

_____

_____

_____

_____

Another living thing

Take responsibility for an animal or plant and take good care of it.

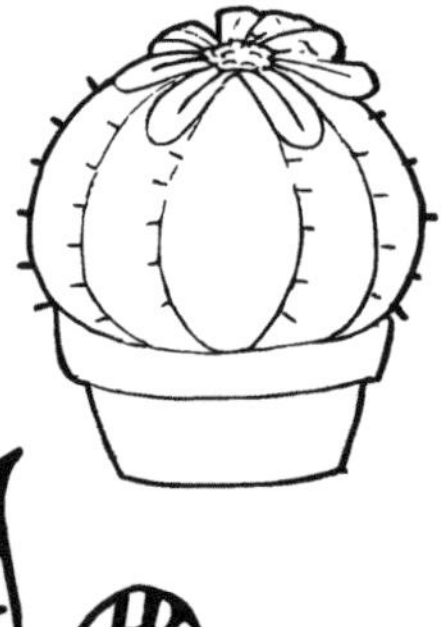

Life is much nicer ...

...without you!

What's more fun without him?

_____

_____

_____

_____

_____

_____

_____

Take farewell

Bury an object or picture that reminds you of him at a place you can visit for mourning.

Choose a place that you do not have to see every day.

Paint your great life without him

You are the helmsman

Do not leave the fears and
negative thoughts in the lead.

You are the helmsman of your life.
Navigate to a happy future where
HE is history!

That's life

If you want to binge-eat, that's perfectly OK.

But keep an eye on your weight and your health.

The 12th month

Today is the ___ . ___ . ___ and you
are feeling _____
How are you now?

_____

_____

_____

_____

_____

_____

_____

Where is your pain and how strong is it?

The 12th month

When did you last contact him?
How did it go?

_____

_____

_____

_____

_____

_____

_____

_____

When did you last see him?
How was it?

_____

_____

_____

_____

_____

When did you last think of him?
How often do you still think of him?

_____

_____

_____

You are lovely

You are great and you will find someone who deserves your love.

Just because he is not there, your life is not bad. Do not wait for him to knock on your door. Enjoy your life!

Paint his sad life without you

Reinvent yourself

A chapter in your life has come to an end.

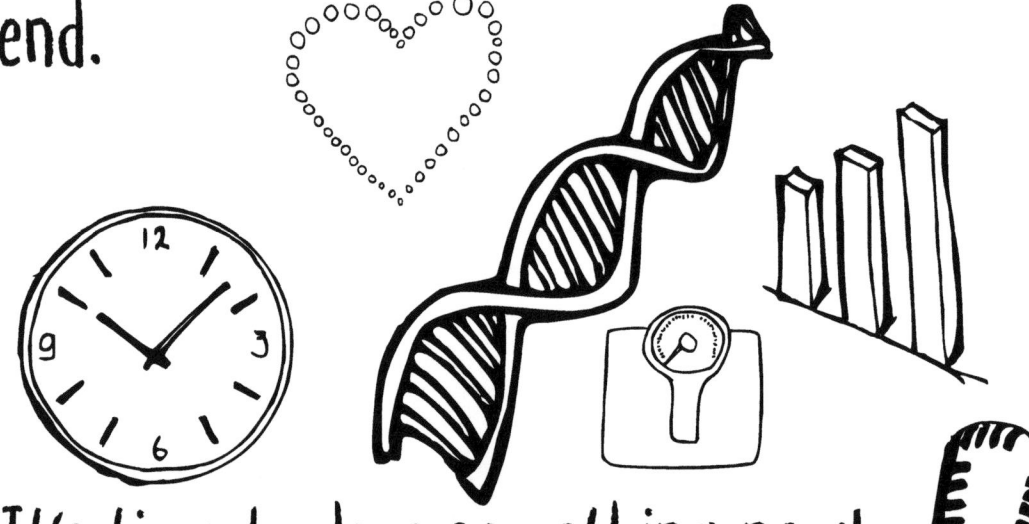

It's time to dare something new! Reinvent yourself. Show everyone that you are even better than before.

Laugh about him

There is something funny about everyone. What is funny about him? Big nose, awful style?

_____

_____

_____

_____

_____

Do not laugh at him! Do not insult him!

Congratulations! ♥ ♥

You have overcome your lovesick on

_____.____._____ (date).

Your lovesickness has lasted

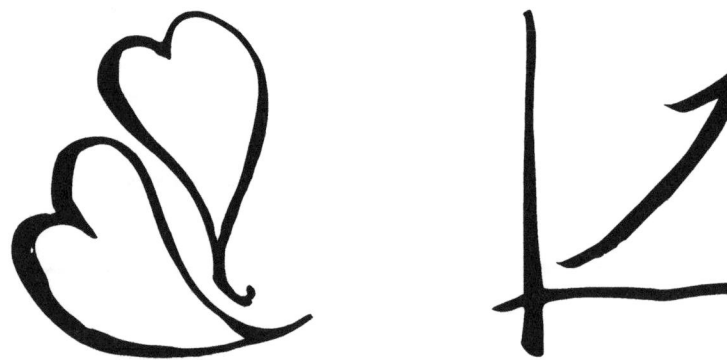

_____.

You are ready for a new love again.

Now, you may insert a picture of him / both of you here as a reminder.

Reminders

Cut out the reminders on the next page and use them as bookmarks.

I am in love with

_____

whom I cannot
have because

_____

_____

_____

_____

_____

_____

_____

_____

_____

I am in love with

_____

whom I cannot
have because

_____

_____

_____

_____

_____

_____

_____

_____

_____

He is your
Mr. Wrong.

He is your
Mr. Wrong.